Tangerine Dre

A YEAR IN

Chelsea Physic Garden

Café Recipes, Garden Photographs and Memorable Dates Diary

Limpet Barron • David Hughes • Sarah Charles

Chelsea Physic Garden was founded in 1673 by The Worshipful Society of Apothecaries of London, in order to train their apprentices in the 'healing arts' and teach them how to identify plants and explore their various uses. The botanist and physician, Sir Hans Sloane (1660-1753), preserved what is now London's oldest botanic garden for future generations when he bought the manor of Chelsea and allowed the apothecaries to lease the 3.8 acre site for a rent of £5. He also encouraged the Garden and its most famous curator, Philip Miller, to introduce new species of plants into cultivation from around the world.

Since then the Garden has become the trial ground for many new foods, such as rhubarb, as well as debating what these plants should be called. Miller and the Swedish botanist, Carl Linnaeus, disagreed over the name of the ubiquitous tomato. Robert Fortune, another past curator, pioneered the use of the Wardian case to transport tea seedlings from China to India, thus expanding the lucrative British tea trade.

Tangerine Dream Café has been providing delicious food at the Garden since 2005. Limpet Barron and David Hughes, along with their talented staff, have enhanced the Garden's reputation for educating people of all ages about the importance of plants in our lives and in particular our health and well-being. While being experimental, Tangerine Dream Café keep their ingredients fresh and their recipes simple, and in this book they let the reader into a few of their secrets.

Rosie Atkins

Curator of Chelsea Physic Garden, London
2002 – 2010

OPPOSITE: The Terrace at Chelsea Physic Garden, where Tangerine Dream Café serve food on public admission days

JANUARY

PREVIOUS PAGES: View looking east over the Traditional Common and Less Common Vegetable Beds, with asparagus forcing jars in the left foreground.
OPPOSITE TOP LEFT: The Swan Walk entrance gate to the Garden, with *Schizophragma hydrangeoides*.
OPPOSITE TOP RIGHT: *Helleborus torquatus*.
OPPOSITE BELOW: View looking south east over the Pharmaceutical Beds.
ABOVE TOP: Arms of the Worshipful Society of Apothecaries of London on the Embankment Gate.
BELOW: A modern replica of a Wardian case.

1

2

3

4

5

6

7

8

9

10

11

12

13

14

As a young doctor, Sloane travelled to the West Indies in 1687 with the newly appointed Governor of Jamaica, the Duke of Albemarle and his wife. It was here that Sloane saw chocolate and milk being mixed together as a drink. He brought back a recipe for this to Britain, that was later marketed under his name.

SIR HANS SLOANE'S ORIGINAL 'HEALTH-GIVING' RECIPE FOR HOT DRINKING CHOCOLATE
"Take A pinte new milke. In a pinte water, & boyle putt in 2 ounces chocolate & 3 ounces sugar, & mill it on ye fyer as aboue & when itt is readyye to boyle upp take it of ye fyre & mix with itt two new layd eggs, but lett your eggs be broke with ye mill in a spoonfull of cold water in a pinte pott, then mix it all to gather & lett it be a little coole as you may drinke it."

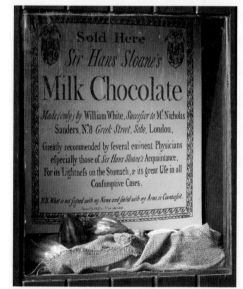

Reproduction of an 18th century 'Sir Hans Sloane Milk Chocolate' advertisement with cocoa pods.
OPPOSITE: Sir Hans Sloane exhibition cart at Chelsea Physic Garden.

PORK LOIN STUFFED WITH PRUNES IN ARMAGNAC

Serves 4
250g Dried Agen Prunes
500ml of Armagnac
1 tenderloin of pork
Salt and pepper
Sage leaves

Place the prunes in a small dish, add the Armagnac and allow them to soak overnight in the fridge.

Pre-heat the oven to 170°C. Slit the tenderloin along its length just under half way through, then make two further shallow cuts at 45 degrees. Looking down the length of the meat you should see a Y-shaped cut. Stuff the loin with three quarters of the prunes and truss securely with string. Save the remaining prunes and Armagnac.

Lightly coat with oil and season with salt and pepper. Add a few sage leaves to the outside of the meat then place in a baking tray incision side up and cover with foil. Cook in the oven for approx 40 mins.

To finish, uncover the meat, turn over and return to the oven at 200°C for approx 8 mins, or until medium brown on the outside. Cut the meat into generous round slices and spoon over a gravy made from a reduction of the left over Armagnac, remaining prunes and meat juices.

A simple country dish that goes well with strong greens, shown here with swiss chard scattered with sprouted amaranthus. We also serve this with spinach, wilted with a clove or two of softened garlic. For those not counting the calories too closely, add a potato and celeriac mash made with cream and butter.

15

16

17

18

19

20

21

22

23

24

25

26

27

28

CHOCOLATE BROWNIES

Makes 32 pieces

500g Amadei 65/70% cocoa solids chocolate, or similar quality and percentage, such as Lindt, broken-up into small pieces

700g caster sugar

80g plain flour (optional)

125g good quality cocoa powder

200g mixed chopped nuts (optional, but recommended)

1 tbsp of Madagascan vanilla essence

8 large free range eggs, lightly beaten

500g melted unsalted butter

Line a 38cm roasting tray with a sheet of baking parchment to overlap on all four sides.

In a large bowl combine all of the dry ingredients, then add the vanilla essence, followed by the beaten eggs, and finally the cooled melted butter. Mix well.

Pour the mixture into the lined roasting tin and bake for 45 mins at 150°C.

The surface should be lightly cracked when ready. Remove and cool for 30 mins, then turn out onto a wire rack and remove the baking parchment.

Cool for a further 20 mins before transferring to a chopping board and cut into 32 equal pieces. Serve with crème fraîche or vanilla ice cream. Stays fresh in an airtight container for up to three days.

The latch to Number 2 Greenhouse by the North Wall.

KEDGEREE

Serves 4

400g long grain rice
200g smoked haddock
200g un-dyed haddock
2 large onions, sliced
2 tbsp melted butter or Indian ghee
2 tbsp olive oil
$1/2$ tsp tumeric powder
$1/2$ tsp ground ginger
$1/2$ tsp garlic powder
$1/2$ tsp ground coriander
2 eggs, only just hardboiled
1 tbsp mix of chopped fresh flat leaf
Parsley and coriander to garnish

Kedgeree originated from the Indian 'khichri', a dish of rice and lentils, which was adapted by resourceful Memsahibs and their cooks to use up leftover provisions. For this reason recipes can vary, but it is an interesting early version of what has now become known as 'fusion' cuisine. This dish makes an excellent brunch.

Set the rice on to cook using twice as much water as rice by volume. Bring to the boil, then simmer until all of the water has been absorbed and the rice is soft and loose when forked through.

Once the rice is on, poach the fish in a 50:50 milk and water mix, cooking until the fish flakes off the skin, but still retains good texture. In a sauté pan, gently cook the sliced onions in the butter and oil, adding the dried spices and herbs to the mix as it softens. Add the flaked fish to the onions after they begin to brown off, and cook for a further 3–4 mins.

Set the rice on individual plates, then ladle on the fish and onion mix, allowing some of the spicy sauce to settle through the rice. Top with egg and the roughly chopped fresh herb mix.

29

30

31

A blackbird perched on a tree in the Garden. The large number of mature trees and water features in the Garden attract a wide variety of native birds.

DARK SEVILLE ORANGE MARMALADE

1.3kg Seville oranges
2 lemons
3.6ltr of water
2.6kg dark brown sugar
2 tbsp black molasses

Cut the fruit in half and juice, retaining the pips. Chop the peel and pulp coarsely, then place in a large pan and cover with water overnight. Drain the pulped peel well. Mix with the fruit juice and water. Tie the pips into a cheesecloth bag and place with the peel and juice mixture in a large pan.

Bring the mixture to the boil over a high heat, then reduce the heat, half cover the pan and simmer for 2 hours or until the peel is soft. Squeeze the contents of the cheesecloth bag out against the side of the pan with a spoon before discarding. Add all the sugar and molasses, stirring slowly with a wooden spoon until it has dissolved. Return to a high heat, boiling rapidly for about 20 mins, or until the setting point has been reached. Skim off any foam and allow to cool for a few minutes before transferring to sterilised jars. Seal with a wax or greaseproof disc, then cover and store in a cool cupboard.

For an extra treat 3–4 tbsp/50ml of whisky may be added to the mixture after the sugar has been added, but before it is boiled up prior to setting.

FEBRUARY

Tangerine Dream Café Tip

HERBS: Picking what is available in the garden and countryside for the salad bowl is a great tonic and all these leaves have restorative qualities. Young dandelion leaves mixed with chopped wild garlic leaves, chervil, comfrey, sorrel, mint and thyme, lightly dressed with olive oil, lemon juice and ground whole black pepper will delight your taste buds and suggest that summer is on its way.

PREVIOUS PAGES: The Woodland Garden: in the foreground, *Helleborus multifidus subsp. hercegovinus*. The tree in the background right is *Tetradium daniellii* with *Aristolochia manshuriensis* and *Galanthus* 'Hill Poe'. OPPOSITE: Snowdrop, *Galanthus* 'Magnet'. ABOVE: Snowdrop, *Galanthus* 'Ginn's Imperati'.

1

2

3

4

5

6

7

8

9

10

11

12

13

14

STEAK WITH ROASTED BEETS AND PORTOBELLO MUSHROOM

Per serving
Baby purple and golden beets
20ml olive oil, 20ml honey, mixed
Salt, pepper & thyme
1 large Portobello mushroom
1 rib eye steak, fresh oregano
Horseradish Cream
50g of fresh fine grated horseradish root
200ml crème fraîche, 20ml red wine vinegar

Trim the beets and boil until just undercooked (a sharp knife will go in, but the beet remains firm). Drain, transfer to a baking tray and paint with the olive oil and honey mix. Add a few sprigs of thyme and cook in the oven for a further 10–15 mins at 150°C. Remove the steak from the fridge 15–20 mins before it's needed, allowing it to come up to room temperature.

Place the mushroom cap-side down on a baking tray, pour a generous shot of olive oil into the gills, add salt, pepper and a little thyme. Cook for 10-12 mins at 150°C until dark and soft. Leave both the beets and mushroom in the cooling oven to keep warm.

Oil and generously season the steak. Fry on a hot (preferably heavy based) grill pan. For a steak around 1.5cm thick, 3 mins before turning over for another 2.5 mins will give a medium finish. Adjust the time according to how you like your steak. Allow the meat to rest for 5 mins.

For the horseradish cream: add the red wine vinegar and approx three tablespoons crème fraîche to the horseradish root. Blend with the spoon until smooth, adding more crème fraîche if required.

Trim the steak of any excess fat and cut into generous strips at an angle, revealing the colour of the meat. Stack the strips into a small mound, interspersed with chopped beets. Top with the Portobello mushroom, a few dabs of the horseradish cream and a light drizzle of oil and the fresh oregano.

Serve with a simple mixed leaf salad of your choice. This dish will stand quite strong flavoured additions such as watercress or fresh peppery rocket.

ABOVE: *Iris* 'Katharine Hodgkin'.
LEFT: *Clivia miniata*.
BELOW: Each plant label has the Latin botanical name. Some labels also give a common or English name. Most botanical names consist of two words, the genus and the species e.g. *Hedera helix*. This binomial system of naming, in which each name consists of two parts, was devised by Linnaeus, the famous 18th century Swedish botanist.

PICKLED BEETS

6 medium sized or 10 small uncooked purple and/
or golden beets
Cold water to cover
375ml red wine vineger
1 1/2 tsp mustard powder
1 tsp rock salt
150g sugar
2 tsp dill seeds
2 meduim onions, thinly sliced

For this dish, using both purple and golden beets
creates a more attractive looking pickle. Cover the
beets with water and boil until tender, drain and set
aside, reserving 375ml of the liquid. When beets have
cooled, remove skin (it should come off easily), the
top and any remaining root cord. Slice into approx
5mm wide discs. In a meduim sized saucepan bring
the beet liquid and the vinegar to the boil, then add
the rest of ingredients with the exception of the dill
seeds. Once again bring contents to the boil, then
remove the pan from the heat.

Put the sliced beets and dill seeds into preserving
jars, then slowly pour the cooled liquid over the
beets until they are covered. Seal the jars and
refrigerate. Allow to steep for a few days before
serving. Serve cold with salads or cooked meats.
Will keep for six weeks in a cool place, refrigerate
when opened.

15

16

17

18

19

20

21

22

23

24

25

26

27

28/29

PINEAPPLE TARTE TATIN

1 pineapple
50g butter
2 tbsp caster sugar
20ml water
500g puff pastry

Remove outer skin from the pineapple, then slice horizontally into five slices and decore. Keep one intact circle of pineapple for your centrepiece, the rest can be cut into halves.

Melt the butter in a large hot frying pan that can also be used in the oven (no plastic handles). Quickly add caster sugar to the melted butter before it browns excessively.

First place the whole pineapple circle in the centre of a 38cm heavy bottom pan, arranging the remaining pieces decoratively around it.

Sprinkle the water around the pan to crisp up the melting butter and the added sugar, producing a toffee-like mixture.

Cook for around 5–8 mins on a medium to high heat, until the toffee mix is beginning to darken. Then cover the top of your pan with the rolled-out puff pastry, tucking in any loose edges around the sides.

Place the pan in a pre-heated oven at 200°C for 15 mins, or until the pastry has risen, turning a rich golden brown, crisped and darker in the centre.

Remove the pan with care, as the handle will be very hot, and in one swift movement turn out the tart, pineapple side up, onto a large plate.

Do this over a sink if possible, and take very good care not to let any stray toffee fall onto exposed skin. Allow to cool slightly, to help set the top.

Then tuck in. Crème fraîche on the side and a good coffee are ideal accompaniments.

Pineapples (*Ananas comosus*) were grown at the Garden in the 18th century, using hotbeds of tanners' bark.

MARCH

Tangerine Dream Café Tip

RHUBARB: Pictured above is rhubarb *Rheum rhaponticum* with a forcing pot. Rhubarb forcing is thought to have first been used in Britain at the Garden around 1817, it produces earlier and more tender stems.

Rhubarb is a beautiful looking fruit with a rich contrast of rose red and bright green colouring. Although the leaves are toxic, the stalks have both medicinal and culinary uses. In warm climates it will grow all year, but in England unless you grow it under dark shed cover, early rhubarb will only be achieved by using forcing jars. These containers can be terracotta (like those at the Garden) or old buckets will do. They are slipped over the early shoots as they appear in spring.

Cut the rhubarb into 5cm lengths, place in a roasting tray, sprinkle with caster sugar and white wine, cover and cook for 20 mins at 150°C. Use in crumbles, tarts, or serve with ice cream.

PREVIOUS PAGES: Looking through to the Curator's House built in 1902. In the foreground, Judas Tree *Cercis siliquastrum*. The tree behind is common or black mulberry *Morus nigra*.
OPPOSITE: The Monocotyledon Beds showing bamboos, *Phyllostachys nigra*, *Himalayacalamus falconeri*, and *Chusquea culeou*, *Thamnocalamus tessellatus* and *Yushania anceps*. The tall palm is *Trachycarpus fortunei*.

1

2

3

4

5

6

7

8

9

10

11

12

13

14

CHICKEN TAGINE

Serves 6

3 large red onions, finely chopped

3 large white onions, finely chopped

2–3 cloves garlic, finely chopped

50g butter

50ml olive oil

2 tsp ground cumin

1 tbsp ground ginger

$^1/_2$ tsp saffron threads

1 tbsp plain flour seasoned with salt and pepper

8 chicken pieces, breast and thigh mix

Small handful of mixed olives

4 roughly chopped preserved lemons

Salt and freshly ground black pepper

2 tbsp fresh coriander, chopped

2 tbsp fresh parsley, chopped

750 ml mix of water and chicken stock

6 artichoke hearts

500g couscous, prepared according to the instructions on the packet

To decorate, chopped mint, pistachio nuts and fresh pomegranate seeds

Gently cook the onions and garlic in the butter and oil in a large casserole dish or pot until soft, then add the spices. While waiting, lightly dust the chicken pieces in seasoned flour and brown off in a heavy pan.

Add the chicken, olives, preserved lemons and half of the fresh herbs to the pot, together with the water and chicken stock mix, which should cover the chicken pieces. Bring to the boil, then simmer for 30 mins.

Add the artichokes and stir in the balance of the fresh herbs. Ensure that the chicken is still covered by the liquid, and simmer for another 30 mins, or until the meat is very tender.

Serve on a bed of couscous, and finish with a scattering of the chopped mint, pistachio nuts and fresh pomegranate seeds.

TOP: View across the Vegetable and Fibre Beds, looking towards the ticket kiosk and Swan Walk entrance.
ABOVE: Set just outside the Swan Walk entrance gate, this stone marks the Garden's links to the Society of Apothecaries of London.
LEFT: Mimosa, *Acacia dealbata*.

Tangerine Dream Café Tip

EGGS: Buy the best eggs you can and store them in a cool place out of direct sunlight. When peeling a boiled egg, a small amount of vinegar in cold water will help, especially when dealing with quails eggs. Put the boiled eggs in the cold water for 20 mins after cooking and they will peel easily. For best results, bring your eggs up to room temp before use, especially for the lighter cake mixes.

ABOVE: Old seed drawers in the gardeners' store.

15

16

17

18

19

20

21

22

23

24

25

26

27

28

TUNISIAN CITRUS AND ALMOND CAKE – FANNY'S CAKE

60g fresh breadcrumbs
120g ground almonds
1 tsp baking powder
Zest of 1 orange, 1 lime and 1 lemon
210ml sunflower oil
4 large free range eggs

Syrup
Juice of 1 orange, 1 lime and $\frac{1}{2}$ lemon
75g golden caster sugar
1 cinnamon stick
2 star anise
3 cardamom pods

Place all the dry ingredients together in a mixer bowl. Add the grated zest of the citrus fruit. Whisk the oil and eggs together in a separate bowl. Starting at a slow speed, allow the dry ingredients to combine before adding the egg and oil mixture. Then increase the speed to thoroughly beat the batter, scraping down the sides once or twice as required.

Pour the mixture into a well oiled 22cm spring form cake tin. Place in a cold oven. Set temp to 190°C and bake for 20 mins. Rotate cake and cover with oiled tin foil, then bake for a further 30 mins, or until a testing skewer comes out clean.

For the syrup: cook all the ingredients together until the syrup is just beginning to brown. Remove from the heat and reserve the cinnamon, star anise and cardamom.

When the cake is nearly cool pierce the top with a skewer at approx 3cm intervals, particularly around the edges. Drizzle the syrup evenly over the surface of the cake. Allow the first application of syrup to be absorbed, then apply a second measure.

Decorate with the reserved cinnamon, star anise and cardamom, and serve with Greek yogurt and fresh raspberries, when in season.

Photographed with leaves of *Eucalyptus leucoxylon* subsp. *megalocarpa* 'Rosea'.

WELSH RAREBIT

Makes 10–12 slices, enough for a family high tea

375g strong cheddar

65ml English beer (try Badgers Tanglefoot or similar)

50ml double cream

1tsp mustard powder

Worcestershire sauce

3 leeks

50ml melted oil and butter mix

1 tsp of caster sugar

Several slices of stoneground or other rustic bread

Grate the cheese, then warm the beer in a pan – do not allow to boil. Mix the mustard powder to a smooth paste with a little cold water, then add the mustard, three shakes Worcestershire sauce and grated cheese to the pan. Stir until it forms a lumpy mix. Set aside and keep warm.

Slice and wash only the pale white end of the leeks discarding the tough upper leaves. Fry in the oil and butter mix on a low to medium heat until soft, adding the sugar half way through the process. Set aside.

Lightly toast the bread on both sides, then lay on a baking tray. Liberally spoon the cheese mix onto the toast, add a shake of Worcestershire sauce onto each slice, then grill until browned. Serve garnished with the sweetened leeks. A simple salad of fresh leaves will perfectly complement the richness of this dish.

Perennial Greens in the Less Common Vegetable Beds. A very small number of familiar vegetables are now grown in the UK, many more unusual varieties of vegetables were grown in the past.

Tangerine Dream Café Tip

PASSION FRUIT SALAD DRESSING

100ml olive oil
30ml white wine vinegar
$^1/_2$ tsp Dijon mustard
1 tbsp fresh basil
Juice and seeds of 1 passion fruit

Combine all the ingrediants in a lidded jam jar and shake well. Add sea salt and ground pepper to taste.

BELOW: A long view across the Systematic Order Beds with a painting by Julian Barrow in the foreground.

29

30

31

APRIL

CAPE GOOSEBERRY CHUTNEY

2 tbsp vegetable oil
$^1/_2$ tsp mustard seeds
$^1/_2$ tsp cumin seeds
4 tbsp chopped onion
1 tsp chopped fresh ginger root
1 tsp chopped green chilli
$^1/_2$ tsp hot dried red chilli (often sold
as chilli flakes)
$^1/_2$ tsp ground cumin
$^1/_2$ tsp ground coriander
Pinch of salt
500g Cape gooseberries, hulled
$^1/_2$ tsp raw cane sugar

Heat the oil, then add the mustard and cumin seeds. After the mustard seeds have started to splutter, add the chopped onion and cook until softened and translucent.

Next, add the ginger root and green chilli and cook for 2–3 mins on a medium heat. Add the red chilli, ground spices and salt, then reduce to a low heat. Spoon the gooseberries and sugar into the mix, and gently sauté for a few minutes, ensuring the fruit retains its shape and does not collapse.

Allow to cool and serve as an accompaniment to oily fish or cheeses.

PREVIOUS PAGES: Looking southwest across the Garden to a copy of a statue of Sir Hans Sloane, by Michael Rysbrack, commissioned by the Society of Apothecaries of London in 1733 in order "That their Successors and Posterity may never forget their Common Benefactor". The original is on loan to the British Museum.
OPPOSITE ABOVE: The blossom of the plum, *Prunus domestica* 'Early Orleans'.
OPPOSITE BELOW: Bulb Frame.

1

2

3

4

5

6

7

8

9

10

11

12

13

14

LAMB CUTLETS AND GREEK SALAD

Serves 4
2 racks of lamb cutlets, French trimmed
1 tsp cracked black pepper
1 tsp coarse sea salt

Greek Salad
1 cucumber, cubed
Half a medium sized red onion, sliced
15–20 baby plum tomatoes
300g Feta cheese, crumbled
1 finely chopped preserved lemon
2 tsp dried oregano

Salsa Verde
65ml olive oil and 10ml red wine vinegar, mixed
Handful of basil, parsley and mint
6 Nonperiel (small) capers
Half a clove of garlic
1 salted anchovy fillet or 6 black olives

Lightly coat the lamb with oil and a generous dusting of cracked black pepper and coarse sea salt and put in an oven-proof hot pan on a hob. Brown both sides and base, skin and fat side down first, before transferring the pan to a hot oven at 200°C. Cook for 15–17 mins for rare, 20 mins for medium and 22–25 mins for well done.

Remove from the heat and cover with a thick cloth then allow to stand for 10 mins before dividing into portions of three or four cutlets each.

For the Greek salad: gently mix the cucumber, onion and tomatoes together then arrange in a small mound on a plate. Crumble the Feta cheese over the top of the mixture, followed by the preserved lemon and dried oregano.

For the Salsa Verde: chop and mix together the ingredients with the oil and vinegar mix.

To serve, divide the Greek salad onto four plates. Place three or four cutlets in a pyramid-shape over the salad. Add a little extra green salad to one side, along with a spoonful of Salsa Verde.

Camomile/Herbal Teas: Camomile infusion or tea is said to ease aches, be a great comforter and promote peaceful sleep. Pre-heat the teapot, add a handful of camomile flowers and pour on boiling water. Let steep for 4-5 mins, then pour. Sweeten to taste. Most other herbal teas are brewed from the leaves of the plant. Mint is very popular in Morocco where sugar is placed in the pot with the leaves. Rosemary is reputed to stimulate the memory, whilst Sage soothes a sore throat. Herbal teas are refreshing and caffeine-free.

OPPOSITE ABOVE: The Auricula Theatre dedicated to Dr David Jamison (1924-2003) who founded the charity which took over Chelsea Physic Garden in 1983. Plant theatres first came to Britain in the 18th century. OPPOSITE BELOW: A view over the Herb Beds. ABOVE: *Paeonia mascula* subsp. *triternata*.

15

16

17

18

19

20

21

22

23

24

25

26

27

28

CRUNCHY LEMON CAKE

Cake Mix
250g butter
200g caster sugar
250g self raising flour
4 large free range eggs
1 tsp baking powder
Zest and juice of 1 medium/large
Amalfi or unwaxed lemon

Topping
Juice of 1 Amalfi or unwaxed lemon
Granulated sugar

Cream the butter and sugar, add half the flour together with the eggs, then blend. Add the rest of the flour, the baking powder, and finally the lemon zest and juice.

Pour into a 38mm loaf tin that has been lined with lightly greased baking paper (not needed if a silicone 'tin' is used). Bake at 150°C for around 50 mins. All ovens vary slightly, and you are looking for a gently risen loaf-like structure that has achieved a medium golden brown colour. You will often see a small fissure down the middle where the risen part has gently separated.

Allow to cool in the tin, and whilst cooling hand blend the juice of the remaining lemon with sufficient granulated sugar to form a thick but liquid syrup. Turn out the cake whilst still a little warm and spoon the topping mix liberally over the top.

Tip: this cake is best on the day, but will keep for a couple of days in an airtight container. It will also freeze. After defrosting, gently warm in the oven before serving.

TRADITIONAL PORK PIE

Serves 4–6
Pastry
450g plain flour, salt and freshly ground
black pepper, 150g lard, 50ml milk, 50ml
water, 1 free range egg, beaten for the
glaze

Pork Jelly
900g pork bones, 2 pigs trotters, 1 large
carrot chopped, 2 sticks celery chopped,
1 bouquet garni, 15 peppercorns,
1tsp anchovy essence

Pie Filling
400g pork shoulder, 200g in approx
1cm cubes, 200g fine chopped or minced,
75g pork belly, skin removed, fine chopped
or minced, 50g lean bacon fine chopped,
1/2 onion, 1 small Cox's apple, 1/2 tsp
ground allspice, 1/2 tsp grated nutmeg,
5 chopped sage leaves, 3 tsp chopped
parsley

For the pastry: Sieve the flour into a large bowl,
add a good pinch of salt and pepper. Melt the
lard with the milk and water over a low heat,
and add to the flour. Knead until the mixture
comes together to form a dough. Wrap in cling
film and chill in the fridge for at least an hour.

For the jelly: Place all of the ingredients in a
large pan and just cover with water. Bring to
the boil then reduce to a simmer for two hours,
periodically skimming off any scum that rises
to the surface. Strain the stock through a sieve to
remove all of the solids, then return to the pan,
set on medium heat and reduce stock to approx
500ml.

For the filling: Combine all the ingredients in
a large bowl, mixing well by hand. Add salt and
pepper to taste.

Roll out the pastry to a thickness of approx
8mm, using three quarters to line the cases,
saving the rest to make the tops.

Line a high sided oven proof dish, or
individual muffin tins with the pastry, then
add the appropriate quantity of filling, shaped
into a ball. Shape the remaining pastry to form
the lids as required. Brush the inner top of the
pastry sides with beaten egg and press the lid on,

pinching together to form a good seal. Brush all the visible pastry with beaten egg, then bake for 45 mins to 1 hour at 180°C or until the pie top is golden brown and slightly risen. When cool, make a small hole in the top, gently warm the jelly, sufficient only to make it pourable, then pour through the hole to carefully top up your pie. Chill in the fridge until the jelly is set.

A great picnic stalwart, and delicious served with homemade Pickled Beets (page 23), Cape Gooseberry Chutney (page 41) or Piccalilli (page 113).

BELOW: An easterly view over the Less Common Vegetable Beds.

29

30

MAY

1

2

3

4

5

6

7

PREVIOUS PAGES: Flowering white for two weeks, fragrant Himalayan musk rose, *Rosa brunonii* scrambles up a *Catalpa bignonioides*.
OPPOSITE: The statue of Sir Hans Sloane surrounded by a collection of plants from Chile including: *Puya coerulea* var. *violacea*, *P. alpestris* and *P. berteroana*.
ABOVE: Sundial on the wall adjacent to the shop.
BELOW: The bright red poppies, *Papaver orientale* var. *bracteatum*, source of an ingredient used in the production of codeine.

8

9

10

11

12

13

14

SEA BASS WITH POTATO, BLACK OLIVE & TOMATO AL FORNO

Per serving
Al Forno
3 par boiled waxy potatoes,
sliced lengthways
2 or 3 plum vine tomatoes, halved
6 black olives marinated in
herb oil (not brine)
1 sprig of rosemary
Splash of olive oil
1 sea bass fillet
Selection of salad leaves
2 or 3 tomatoes
Pesto sauce (see page 57)

For the al Forno: place the potatoes, tomatoes and olives on a baking tray. Strip the leaves from the rosemary sprig and scatter over the mix, cover with a drizzle of olive oil and cook for 12–15 mins at 180°C.

Pat the sea bass fillet dry, drizzle on some olive oil to the skin side then season. Cook skin side down for 4 mins in a hot griddle pan that has been pre-oiled to prevent sticking. The edge of the skin should be browning at this stage. Turn over and cook for a further 1–2 mins.

To serve, layer the plate firstly with a selection of salad leaves, followed by the al Forno, then finally the fish, skin side up with a portion of pesto sauce (see recipe page 57). Add a wedge of lemon if desired.

15

16

17

18

19

20

21

PESTO SAUCE

75g pine nuts
1 large bunch of basil, approx 100g
1 tbsp parsley
75g Parmesan, fine grated
175g good olive oil
Clove of garlic, chopped
Salt and pepper to taste

This is a very easy and satisfying sauce to make.
Place the pine nuts, basil, parsley, garlic, half the
Parmesan and oil in a food processor and coarsely
chop. Add more oil and Parmesan until you have
a smooth mix. Taste and add salt and pepper as
desired. This is very often served with pasta, it also
goes well with our sea bass dish.
(See recipe page 54)

OPPOSITE ABOVE: A Stevenson Screen housing
weather measuring instruments. Data is collected here
for the Meteorological Office, including; air temperature,
humidity, dewpoint and atmospheric pressure. The plant
to the right of the station is 'Apothecaries' rose *Rosa
gallica* var. *officinalis*.
OPPOSITE BELOW LEFT: The bean *Vicia faba*.
OPPOSITE BELOW RIGHT: Horseradish *Armoracia
rusticana*.

22

23

24

25

26

27

28

RUM BABA

250g plain flour
2 large free range eggs
Good pinch salt
1 tbsp tepid milk
1 tsp fresh yeast
30g melted butter

Syrup
200ml water
150g caster sugar
40ml dark rum
Cream and cherries
(12 small metal pudding bowls)

Place the flour, eggs and salt in a mixing bowl. Using a mixer with a dough hook, knead the contents on a medium speed, adding the milk and yeast as the initial mixture begins to combine. When you have a semi smooth mix, add the butter. From the start, this process will take 15–20 mins.

Cover the bowl and allow to rest at room temperature for 30 mins. Divide into 12 balls, cover and rest for a further 10 mins. Carefully place the risen dough into the lightly greased small metal pudding bowls and bake at 140°C for 40 mins or until well risen and thoroughly cooked through.

For the syrup: combine the water with the sugar in a pan, bring to the boil then simmer for a few minutes until the liquid begins to thicken slightly, adding 40ml of dark rum half way through the process.

Soak the Babas in the syrup, draining off the excess. Cover and refrigerate. Serve as shown with cream and a cherry on top, or a mix of Chantilly cream sweetened with fresh fruit.

ABOVE: Peppermint, *Mentha x piperita.*

LEFT: The Pond Rockery. Originally built in 1773 as just a rockery, it subsequently had a pond added and is now a Grade 11 listed structure. Constructed of materials from many sources including volcanic rock from Sir Joseph Banks' expedition to Iceland in 1771, a giant clam shell from his South Pacific expedition with Captain Cook on the Endeavour 1768-1771 and various stones from the Tower of London.
The waterlily is *Nymphaea alba*.
BELOW: A view of the Pond Rockery planted with predominately Mediterranean and Atlantic Island plants, including Cretan endemics such as *Petromarula pinnata*.

29

30

31

ABOVE: A bust of Sir Joseph Banks, on the Pond Rockery, surrounded by *Stachys tymphaea* and *Santolina chamaecyparissus*.
BELOW: *Echium wildpretii* subsp. *trichosiphon* alongside stonework in the Pond Rockery.

JUNE

STRAWBERRY JAM

3 kg of strawberries, topped & hulled
Juice of 2 Amalfi or unwaxed lemons
2 kg preserving sugar
Pinch of black pepper
Kilner or similar jars for bottling
Waxed paper discs to cover jam

Put the strawberries and lemon juice into a large stockpot or saucepan. Simmer until the fruit is soft, stirring frequently. Add sugar and stir over a medium heat until the sugar dissolves and combines with the fruit. Be careful not to use too high a heat initially to avoid burning the mixture.

Add the pepper, turn up the heat, then when the surface is liquid and the sugar appears clear, boil for a further 10–12 mins, stirring occassionally.

Test the readiness of the mixture by placing about half a teaspoon of jam on a cold side plate and allow to cool for 2–3 mins. Tilt the plate to about 45 degrees. If the jam is ready and sets, a skin will have formed on the surface, and it will not slide down the plate. If it is not ready and does not set, return the jam to the heat and continue to boil for a few more minutes before checking again.

Fill sterilised jars with the warm jam, cover the top with the waxed paper discs, then seal the jars. Delicious with homemade scones and clotted cream.

Please note, jam needs to be properly boiled, gentle simmering will not do.

PREVIOUS PAGES: *Echium pininana* seen along the Macaronesian borders next to the Garden's Swan Walk entrance.
OPPOSITE: The Curator's House covered with *Rosa banksiae*. The tall shrub on the left is *Carmichaelia stevensonii*.

1

2

3

4

5

6

7

8

9

10

11

12

13

14

Asparagus, Prosciutto and Soft Boiled Egg

Per serving
7 asparagus stems, use English in season
Salt and pepper to taste
20ml olive oil
1 large free range egg
Mixed endive, rocket and oak leaf salad
1 slice of best prosciutto ham
Fresh Parmesan shavings

Trim the asparagus to remove the woody and dry end. Cook in lightly salted boiling water for approx 4 mins until tender. Drain and dress with either butter or olive oil as preferred. Soft boil an egg, this can be started once you have the asparagus on. You can use the same pan if there is sufficient space, add the egg approx 1 min after the asparagus.

Place a small quantity of the mixed salad on a medium sized plate, then add the asparagus spears in a criss cross pattern, placing the lightly folded slice of prosciutto on top of the spears.

Carefully peel the egg, place on the prosciutto then slice in half allowing the yolk to run free. Dress with a small quantity of the Parmesan cheese. Season to taste.

Makes a light meal or perfect starter.

ABOVE: The exotic bean *Phaseolus coccineus* 'Black Night'.
LEFT: Tomato, *Solanum lycopersicum* 'Costoluto Fiorentino'.
BELOW: Asparagus peas, *Tetragonolobus purpureus*.
Philip Miller, gardener at Chelsea Physic Garden from 1722 to 1770, is thought to have been the first in Great Britain to recommend eating runner beans.

15

16

17

18

19

20

21

WATERMELON SALAD

Serves 12–16
1 red onion
2 limes
1 sweet watermelon
5 × 200g blocks of Feta cheese, cubed
Provençale herb marinated black olives
40g flat leaf parsley
Good quality Tuscan or Greek virgin olive oil will
compliment the flavours

Thinly slice the onion, and cover with the squeezed lime juice, then place in the fridge overnight. This will turn the onion a subtle pink colour, giving a good citrussy counterpoint to the flavour of the Feta cheese. The longer you leave them the more they will colour, so two or three days is fine.

Cube the watermelon then place in a large bowl. Add the Feta, then top with a generous scattering of whole parsley leaves.

Finish by adding the marinated onions and olives, plus a liberal dose of good, strong, fruity olive oil. We would recommend Tuscan or Greek oil for this dish to best compliment the flavours.

ABOVE: David Hughes with the finished salad standing in front of *Olea europaea* subsp. *europaea*. This is the largest Olive tree growing out of doors in England.

22

23

24

25

26

27

28

LAVENDER SCONES

Makes 12
250g self-raising flour
1 1/2tsp baking powder
100g caster sugar
2tsp dried or fresh English
lavender (*Lavandula angustifolia*)
110g butter
Juice of 1/2 a lemon
200ml milk at room temperature

Mix the dry ingredients in a bowl with the lavender. Rub through the butter to form a fine breadcrumb mix. Add the lemon juice and milk at the same time. The mixture should be quite wet once blended.

Tip it onto a well-floured board, flour your hands and then knead the mixture for about 30 seconds until it is floured enough to work with. It should remain moist on the inside.

Shape into a flattish round about 2cm thick. Cut into shapes with a floured cutter. Bake in a preheated oven at 160°C for 12–15 mins. Remove and leave to cool on a wire rack.

Serve with homemade strawberry jam (see recipe page 65), greengage, blackcurrant or mirabelle jam and clotted cream.

BELOW: *Lavandula angustifolia.*

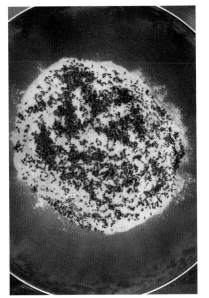

Amalfi Lemonade

Makes approximately two 1.75ltr jugs
6–7 Amalfi or large unwaxed lemons,
(choose the best quality fresh lemons)
500g caster sugar or more according to
taste

Peel the skin off the lemons in large strips with a good paring knife. Be careful to take as little of the pith as possible.

Place peel in a heatproof basin and cover with boiling water for about 4–5 mins. This releases the oil from the lemon rind and provides a wonderful aroma.

Next, juice all the lemons, and add the juice to the bowl with the peel.

Add sugar; these lemons will take a surprising amount. Start with 500g, then top up with a little more boiling water to dissolve the sugar.

Lastly add cold water to make just under 3 litres. The lemonade should have a slightly sherbert zing, and be on the sweet side of how you like it to taste.

Then add more sugar to taste, and top up to 3.5 litres. Place in the refrigerator to steep overnight, which allows the flavour to develop. Serve chilled.

OPPOSITE ABOVE: Three stages in the preparation of Amalfi Lemonade.
OPPOSITE BELOW: A basket of Amalfi lemons from Italy.
BELOW: *Citrus limon*.

29

30

JULY

1

2

3

4

5

6

7

PREVIOUS PAGES: Looking northeast over the
Common Vegetable Beds towards the *Laurus nobilis*.
This is a similar view to the opening picture in January
and makes a striking contrast.
OPPOSITE: Ruby chard *Beta vulgaris* subsp. *cicla*, grown
for colour, form and for its delicious flavour.
ABOVE: *Capsicum chinense* 'Dorset Naga', one of the
hottest chillies in the world, measuring over one million
on the Scoville Scale of heat units.
BELOW: Sweet peppers enjoy a summer shower.

8

9

10

11

12

13

14

SALMON EN CROUTE

Serves 4
500g puff pastry
Side of wild salmon
60ml dry semolina
4 stem ginger in syrup, medium chopped
1 tbsp currants
1 beaten egg

A very simple but effective dish to prepare. Roll out the pastry to about 1.5mm thick; you need sufficient to fold around the salmon and seal the edges, plus a little to decorate.

Place on a large baking sheet covered in baking parchment. Coat the salmon base with the semolina, then place on the pastry 2cm from one of the longer edges.

Evenly cover the salmon top with the stem ginger and currants, then fold over the pastry to seal in the fish. Press down the edges firmly, using the rounded tip of a teaspoon or your finger, as preferred. Leaving a 2cm crimped edge, cut off the spare pastry, then roll it out again to use as decoration.

Now comes the creative part. With the spare pastry you can create a professional looking lattice pattern, or try a fish or a mermaid, or something else nautical. Diagonally score the pastry as this lets the steam out and keeps it crisp, apply your pastry design, then brush all of the top with the beaten egg.

Cook in the oven at 180°C for 25 mins, or until the pastry has risen and is a rich golden brown colour. Delicious with green beans, asparagus or a mixed salad.

15

16

17

18

19

20

21

Scotch Egg

Makes 5
450g sausage meat (combine 325g pork mince
with 125g fine chopped streaky bacon and season)
Alternatives: use a ready-made mix from your
butcher, or de-skin a few of your favourite sausages
1 tsp fresh thyme leaves, finely chopped
1 tbsp fresh parsley leaves, roughly chopped
3 sage leaves, finely chopped
1 medium red onion, finely chopped
5 large free range eggs, soft boiled, de-shelled
100g seasoned flour
2 beaten eggs
125g breadcrumbs

Combine the sausage meat, herbs and red onion and
mix well. Divide into five equal quantities and on a
floured board press into five oval shapes, sufficient
to wrap around the eggs. With floured hands, lightly
dredge the eggs in the seasoned flour before evenly
covering them in the sausage meat and sealing the
edges. Brush with beaten egg, then roll them in the
breadcrumbs. This may be done twice to achieve a
slightly thicker and crunchier coating.

Deep fry in a pan of vegetable oil at 185°C for
6–8 mins, or until a dark golden brown all over. If
you don't have a suitable thermometer, heat the oil
until a breadcrumb will sizzle in the pan, browning
within a minute. You may also shallow fry the eggs,
but they need to be turned several times to ensure
the meat is evenly cooked. Adjust cooking times to
suit. Allow to cool before serving.

OPPOSITE ABOVE LEFT: x *Amarygia parkeri* 'Alba'.
OPPOSITE ABOVE RIGHT: Fruit from the pomegranate
tree, *Punica granatum*, one of the oldest plants in
the Garden.
OPPOSITE BELOW: A bed with less common culinary
herbs and vegetable plants.

22

23

24

25

26

27

28

SUMMER PUDDING

Serves 8
500g mixed summer fruits
125g caster sugar
284ml red wine
8–10 thin slices of day old white bread
A few summer berries to finish
Clotted cream
(8 small metal pudding basins, lined with cling film)

Bring the fruit and sugar to the boil in the red wine, strain and reserve the juice. Allow the juice to cool until tepid.

Line each basin with cling film and leave some overhanging the edge. This will help with getting the puddings out once they are ready to serve.

Remove the crusts from the bread. Cut eight small circles to fit the bases and eight larger circles to fit the tops. Dip the smaller circles in the juice and place them juice side down in the bottom of the basins. Line the sides of the basins with more dipped bread. Ensure the bread fits together well, overlapping if necessary.

Fill each basin with the fruit, then top off with the larger circles of dipped bread. Fold the overhanging cling film over the base, then chill in the fridge for 3 hours.

Turn out and decorate with fresh berries. Serve with a spoonful of clotted cream.

BELOW: *Fragaria* x *ananassa* 'Honeoye'.

LEMON POSSET WITH FENNEL SHORTBREAD

Serves 8
Posset
500ml double cream
125g caster sugar
Juice and finely grated zest of
2 unwaxed lemons

Shortbread
250g butter
110g golden or white caster sugar, plus
2-3 tsp for sprinkling
250g plain flour, sifted
110g fine semolina
1tsp crushed fennel seeds

For the posset: place the cream and sugar in a pan and bring to the boil. Simmer for 3 mins. Remove from the heat, stir in the lemon zest and juice and leave to cool. Pour into 4 large Martini glasses then chill in the fridge until set. Decorate with edible flowers, such as nasturtium, violets or pansies.

For the shortbread: put the butter in a mixer and beat until smooth. Add the sugar and beat until creamy, then add the flour, followed by the semolina and crushed fennel seeds. Continue until thoroughly incorporated. Roll out on to a lightly floured clean surface and cut into individual shortbreads with a cookie cutter. Place on a baking sheet covered with baking parchment. Bake for 1 hour in the oven at 150˚C, then sprinkle evenly with caster sugar when removed.

The edible flowers of the nasturtium, *Tropaeolum majus* 'Tip Top Mahogany'.

29

30

31

ABOVE: Angelica, *Angelica archangelica*, is attractive and delicately flavoured with a strong scent. The young stems and leaf stalks can be finely chopped and cooked with trout or sugared and candied for decorative use, whilst the 'seeds' can also be used in cooking.

POTTED SHRIMPS

Serves 6
200g butter
350g small brown shrimps, peeled
1 stick of mace
1/2 tsp freshly grated nutmeg
1/2 tsp cayenne pepper

Clarify half of the butter by gently melting small cubes over a low heat, skimming off any surface scum and gently pouring off the oil which has separated from the milky solids at the bottom of the pan. Set aside the clarified butter, but keep warm and liquid.

Heat the remaining 100g of butter in a medium pan until it has melted, then add the shrimps and spices. Stir carefully until the mix is thoroughly and evenly heated through, taking care not to allow the mixture to boil. Remove the stick of mace and divide the mixture into six small ramekins. Carefully spoon a covering of clarified butter over each one and chill until ready to serve. Traditionally served with a wedge of lemon and some thinly sliced buttered brown toast.

AUGUST

PICKLED GREENGAGES

Makes 4 -5 Kilner jars
2kg firm greengages, washed
Seeds from 20 cardamom pods
2 heaped tsp mace blades
12 dried red chillies
2 tbsp green peppercorns
1 ltr distilled white vinegar
500g granulated or caster sugar

Halve and stone the greengages and pack them into sterilised 500ml Kilner jars. Distribute the spices evenly between the jars. Put the vinegar and sugar into a pan and gently heat to dissolve the sugar, stirring a few times. Bring to the boil for a couple of minutes.

Pour the hot vinegary syrup into the jars, enough to cover the fruit, and seal with vinegar proof lids. Turn the jars upside down for 15 mins, then turn the right way up and allow to cool. Store in a cool dark place for up to six months, or slightly longer if kept in a fridge. Label the jars and include the date you made it and an approximate shelf life.

Serve with cold meats, cheeses and a good glass of red wine.

PREVIOUS PAGES: Hardy banana, Musa basjoo.
OPPOSITE: *Ipomoea lobata* mixed with *I. purpurea* in the Systematic Order Beds.

1

2

3

4

5

6

7

8

9

10

11

12

13

14

GOATS CHEESE, GRUYÈRE AND SUNDRIED TOMATO TARTE

Pastry
250g plain flour
125g unsalted butter
Approx 75ml cold water

Filling
4 large free range eggs
300ml double cream
325g cave-aged Gruyère cheese, grated
280g sundried tomato paste
75g crumbly goats cheese
Chopped fresh chives

For the pastry: pulse the flour and butter in a food processor until it forms breadcrumbs. Then add cold water and pulse until it combines. A slightly wet texture gives stretch and a crispier pastry.

Lightly grease a 28cm loose-bottomed tart tin. Knead the pastry on a floured work surface, roll out until about 2.5 mm thick. Place the pastry in the tin, pressing into the sides, leaving 1cm over the edges. Chill in the freezer for 30 mins. (See pastry tip on page 93.) Bake for 20 mins at 150°C, remove parchment, bake for a further 10 mins until crisp and mid golden brown.

For the filling: whisk the eggs and cream in a bowl until combined. Stir in the grated Gruyère. Spread sundried tomato paste evenly over pastry, pour in the cheese and egg mix. Crumble the goats cheese randomly over the surface and bake for approx 40 mins at 150°C. The filling should be set, and a mottled golden brown. Cool for 10 mins, scatter the top with chopped chives.

ABOVE LEFT: Sunflower,
Helianthus annuus
'Moonwalker'.
ABOVE: Monkey puzzle,
Araucaria araucana.
LEFT: The Matilija poppy,
Romneya coulteri, playing
host to a bee probably
from the Garden's own
hives.

Tangerine Dream Café Tip

15

TART CASES FOR SAVOURY BASES
Use a fork to pierce the base, preventing uneven 'blooming' of the pastry during cooking. Cover the pastry with baking parchment and a handful of ceramic baking beans. Bake for 20 mins at 150°C, remove beans and parchment, bake for a further 10 mins until crisp and mid golden brown. Allow to cool, then add your filling.

16

17

18

ROASTING SEEDS AND NUTS: 350g mixed unsalted nuts and seeds, 1 tbsp of honey, 1tsp dried chilli flakes, 1tsp ground cayenne, 1tsp ground cumin, 2 tbsp olive oil, 1 tsp paprika, 1tsp mix of sea salt and cracked black pepper. Combine ingredients in bowl then lay out on silicone baking sheet set on baking tray. Place in pre-heated oven at 180°C for 20 mins. Cool and store in an airtight jar.

19

20

21

22

23

24

25

26

27

28

PEA, BEAN, GREEN AND YELLOW COURGETTE SALAD

Serves 4
500g fresh garden peas (good quality
frozen will do)
500g broad beans (frozen will do)
3 large green courgettes
3 large yellow courgettes
Handful of fresh mint
Approx 10 slices of prosciutto ham
40g flat leaf parsley
Salt to taste

Cook the peas, beans and courgettes until al
dente. Refresh them in ice cold water to keep
their colour and structure. Place the peas and
beans in a bowl, then cut the courgettes into
rough cubes and add. Chop the mint, add the
olive oil, mix well and add salt to taste.

Grill the prosciutto, then shred by hand
and scatter on top.

Decorate with whole leaves of flat leaf
parsley, lightly oiling to give it an inviting
gloss. A fresh and crunchy light meal.

POTATO, FENNEL AND RADICCHIO SALAD

Serves 4
500g salad new potatoes (see below)
1 fennel head
1 radicchio head
40g parsley
15 olives (optional)

Boil the salad potatoes to just cooked – we
use baby Jersey Royals in season, but Cornish
Mids or Charlottes also work well. Drain and
place in a bowl. Liberally sprinkle with olive
oil and add salt.

Thinly slice the fennel and place on top.
Halve the radicchio and de-core, tearing the
remaining leaves into large uneven pieces.
Scatter on top together with the olives and
lightly toss the salad to just reveal the potatoes.

Dress with the juice of an orange, 60ml
white wine vinegar and 90ml olive oil,
whisked together.

SUMMER FRUIT MERINGUE

100ml egg whites at room temperature
200g caster sugar
Pinch of salt
Dash of vanilla essence added at
the end of the mix

Place all the ingredients into a scrupulously clean bowl and whisk until stiff peaks form, adding the vanilla essence last. Using a large spoon place approx 20 servings on to a baking tray covered with baking paper.

Bake at 120°C for 90 mins to achieve a crisp white meringue with a soft chewy interior.

Serve with whipped cream and summer fruits to your choice.

Egg whites will keep fresh in the fridge for a week in an airtight container, or freeze for up to six weeks.

ABOVE: Blackberry, *Rubus fructicosus*.

29

30

31

FENNEL: Sometimes called Venetian or sweet fennel, the feathery tops are used as a herb, whilst the bulbs can be de-cored, thinly sliced and used raw in salads. Very popular in Italian cookery it can also be boiled, steamed, roasted or braised. We prefer to roast or braise, lightly caramalising to both soften and compliment its aniseed taste.

SODA BREAD

Makes one large loaf
250g plain flour
1 tsp salt
1 1/2 tsp bicarbonate of soda
250g wholemeal flour
150g large oat flakes
1 tbsp clear honey
1 tbsp black treacle
500ml buttermilk

Pre-heat the oven to 200°C, then cover a baking sheet with a piece of baking parchment. Mix all the dry ingredients together. Make a well in the centre for the honey, treacle and buttermilk. Work it together lightly with your hands until you have a loose, wet dough.

Dust your hands with flour and shape the dough into a round. Place in the centre of the parchment and cut a cross into the top with a sharp knife. Cook for around 45 mins, or until the bread sounds hollow when tapped on the base. Transfer to a wire rack and cover with a lightly dampened cloth to cool.

SEPTEMBER

1

2

3

4

5

6

7

QUINCE JELLY

Makes two 300g jars
1.8kg ripe quinces
575ml water
6 bruised allspice berries
Lemon juice (see below)
Preserving sugar (see below)

Peel, core and quarter the fruit. Place the quinces in a large saucepan with the water and the allspice berries. Bring to the boil, then simmer for 40–50 mins until the fruit is very tender. Filter the fruit and accompanying juice through a muslin fruit bag, allowing it to drain into a large pan for at least 12 hours. This needs to be done in a bug and insect free environment!

Transfer the strained juice to a clean pan. For every 450ml of liquid add 30ml lemon juice and 400g of sugar. Place the pan over a low heat, and stir until the sugar is dissolved, then bring to the boil without stirring for approx 25 mins, or until the jelly reaches setting point. The colour does take some time to develop and it may vary by batch. Skim off any surface foam, cool slightly, then transfer to warmed jars and seal. Store in a cool environment.

Quince jelly makes an excellent accompaniment to cheese, especially the harder Spanish cheeses like Manchego.

The quince has been grown in England since Roman times.

PREVIOUS PAGES: Looking north across the lawn in front of the main Chelsea Physic Garden building, the Café is on the ground floor.
OPPOSITE: *Cydonia oblonga*, the common quince situated in the Philip Miller Beds.

8

9

10

11

12

13

14

MONKFISH AND SCALLOP SKEWERS

Serves 4

Purée

200g fresh or frozen peas, 200g adame beans, 50g fresh mint leaves, 85ml olive oil, Pinch of salt

Lentils

500g Puy lentils, 2 garlic cloves
1 large red chilli
2 tsp maple syrup
17ml sherry vinegar
1 tbsp wholegrain Dijon mustard

Skewers

500g skinned and de-boned monkfish fillets, 1 head fennel
8 large Brixham or Scottish scallops
4 long rosemary skewers
Oak leaf, rocket and frizee endive leaves
Pinch of cayenne pepper
8 rough chopped San Mazzano tomatoes

For the purée first, place the peas and beans in salted boiling water for about 4 mins if frozen, 8–10 mins if fresh. Drain and put into a food processor. Add the other ingredients and blend to form a coarse purée.

Cook the lentils in twice their volume of water with the garlic and whole chilli for approximately 20–30 mins. When the water has all but evaporated they should be just slightly nutty. Add the maple syrup, sherry vinegar and Dijon mustard and mix well.

For the skewers: cut the monkfish into 12 good sized cubes. Slice the fennel bulb into batons approx 2cm x 5cm. Thread a piece of monkfish on a rosemary skewer, then a baton of fennel followed by a scallop. Repeat until you have 3 pieces of monkfish and 2 scallops per skewer. Brush with olive oil, a little salt and freshly ground pepper. Brown in a hot pan, then transfer to a hot (200°C) oven for 7–8 mins.

Scatter a few dressed salad leaves on a plate, and part cover with the lentils. Divide the purée into four and place on top of the lentils. Add the skewer, a pinch of cayenne pepper and a spoonful of chopped tomatoes.

Serve with a wedge of lemon. Delicious.

LEFT: Bee hives situated near the Boatyard in the south east corner of the Garden. The area that surrounds them is planted as a Mediterranean woodland.

BELOW: Fortune's Tank Pond at the Thames end of the Garden is home to British native collections. Native seed grown in the foreground is from Dr Miriam Rothschild's stock which includes many cornfield annuals.

Tangerine Dream Café Tip

15

16

17

HONEY – It is known that the ancient Egyptians were using honey in their recipes over 2,000 years ago for many health benefits. Incorporated into the diet it is said to help the body's immune system. Honey is an ideal natural sweetener, richer in taste than sugar and can be used in the kitchen as a glaze for both sweet and savoury dishes.

18

Put a little in French dressing as it helps to bring out all the flavours.

When making a lemon drink as a cold remedy, keep the water at 40°C or below before adding the honey to maximise its healing properties.

19

20

21

ABOVE: Sweet Cicely, *Myrrhis odorata*, is a naturalised British wildflower that was formerly in use as a pot herb.

22

23

24

25

26

27

28

FIG, THYME, ALMOND & HONEY TART

Pastry
125g unsalted butter
340g plain flour
65g icing sugar
3 large free range egg yolks

Filling
250g unsalted butter
250g caster sugar
250g ground almonds
3 large free range eggs
12 purple figs
1 tbsp fresh picked thyme, chopped
1 tbsp runny Chelsea Physic Garden or another English honey

For the pastry: cube the butter and place in a food processor with the flour and pulse until it forms breadcrumbs. Add the icing sugar and egg yolks, then pulse until completely blended. The mixture will be quite soft.

Turn mixture onto a lightly floured work surface and pat into a flat, round patty. Wrap in cling film and refridgerate for two hours.

Grease with a little butter a 28cm loose-bottomed tart tin. Roll out the chilled pastry on a floured surface, then line the tin with the rolled out pastry, easing it into the fluted sides. If it breaks you can press in a small piece to effect repair.

Place in the freezer for one hour, then bake at 150°C for approx 20 mins, or until golden brown. Remove from the oven and allow to cool.

For the filling: cream together the butter and sugar in a food processor.

Add the almonds and eggs, whisk together and pour the mixture into the cooled tart shell.

Slice the figs vertically into 4, not quite cutting all of the way down, then fan them out into a star shape as you place them on to the surface of the mixture.

Sprinkle with thyme then bake at 150°C for 50 mins. Drizzle the honey over the tart and leave to cool before serving with crème fraîche or strained Greek yoghurt.

Tangerine Dream Café Tip

29

30

MULBERRIES: Care must be taken whilst handling as the fruit has a very potent dye, and will stain clothes with a bright purple colour. The fruit makes a delicious crumble and should be served with sugar and cream to taste, or can be eaten freshly picked from the tree.

Cooking the fruit down with an equal amount of caster sugar and 350ml of port creates a sophisticated sauce to use with pan fried pigeon breasts.

Mulberries keep well for 2-3 days in an airtight container in the fridge. If puréed they will freeze well. Serve them with cream and meringues (see recipe on page 96).

The mulberry tree which produces the dark red/ purple fruits is the variety more likely to be found in English gardens and can live for many years. The trees have large limbs which are often supported and branches that sweep down onto the ground, which seem to create their own steadying structure for self support.

OPPOSITE ABOVE: *Amaryllis belladonna* 'Rubra'.
OPPOSITE BELOW LEFT: *Eucomis autumnalis*.
OPPOSITE BELOW RIGHT: *Canna latifolia*.
ABOVE: Black mulberry, *Morus nigra*.
RIGHT: Weeping mulberry, *Morus alba* 'Pendula'.

OCTOBER

The Pharmaceutical Ga

PICCALILLI

2.5 kg of diced fresh vegetables –
cauliflower florets, green and yellow courgettes,
romanesque broccoli, small pickling onions and
de-seeded beef tomatoes make a good base
337g rock salt
1 ltr malt vinegar
1 tbsp tumeric
1 tbsp mustard powder
1 tbsp ground ginger
2–3 cloves of crushed garlic
200g sugar
2–3 tbsp of cornstarch (fine polenta flour
dissolved in water then made into a thin paste will
substitute)

Separate the vegetables into florets or rough cut into approx 2cm chunks as appropriate, then place into a large dish. Cover with the salt for 24 hours, after which they should be rinsed and drained.

Put the rest of the ingredients (except the cornstarch) into a large pan, and bring to the boil. Add the vegetables, and simmer until they are still slightly crunchy. Add a cup or two of a 50:50 water and vinegar mix to cover the vegetables if needed.

The cornstarch and flour mix needs to be added to the pan at this stage and stirred through. Re-boil for 2–3 mins until the liquid has started to thicken. Some adjustment to the cornstarch or flour may be needed if you have had to increase the vinegar to water quantity.

Cool, then decant into preserving jars, and allow to stand for a few days before serving. An ideal accompaniment to cold meats and an interesting addition to smoked fish.

PREVIOUS PAGES: Looking south west across the Pharmaceutical Beds.
OPPOSITE: A Morning Glory, *Ipomoea purpurea* 'Grandpa Otts' growing above pumpkin *Cucurbita pepo*.

1

2

3

4

5

6

7

8

9

10

11

12

13

14

BELUGA LENTIL AND SQUASH SALAD

Serves 4

Large butternut squash

20ml olive oil

Salt and pepper

4g of freshly-picked thyme leaves

500g pack Beluga lentils (try Merchant & Gourmet)

2 cloves of garlic

1 whole red chilli

30ml red wine vinegar

1 tbsp wholegrain Dijon mustard

45ml balsamic vinegar

1 red chilli, de-seeded, finely chopped

1 tbsp of flat leaf parsley, roughly chopped

Remove the outer hard layer of the squash with a potato peeler. Then slice the squash into rings and remove seeds, or cut into cubes. Place on a baking tray. Liberally coat with olive oil, season with salt and pepper, and scatter the thyme over. Place in a pre-heated oven at 160°C for 30–40 mins. When properly cooked the squash should have softened and have blackened very slightly at the edges.

Whilst the squash is cooking, place the lentils in twice their volume of water, with the garlic and chilli. Simmer on a medium heat for around 15 mins or until sufficiently softened, but still with a nutty edge.

Cool, discard the chilli and garlic cloves, then add the red wine vinegar, Dijon mustard and balsamic, mixing well. A small amount of salt may be added to taste.

Put the lentils in a large bowl placing the cooked squash on top, then add the finely chopped chilli and parsley. Dress with a good quality olive oil and serve. Ideal with a green salad.

ABOVE: Aubergine, *Solanum melongena* 'Black Beauty'.
RIGHT: Glasshouses in the north east corner of the
Garden built against the high brick wall.
BELOW RIGHT: Black Tuscan Kale, 'Cavolo Nero di
Toscana'.
BELOW: Chamomile, *Anthemis tinctoria*.

Tangerine Dream Café Tip

MELTING CHOCOLATE: For quality use dark chocolate. Go for a 55–70% cocoa chocolate and melt in a bain marie with about 15% by volume cool water added, stirring constantly on a gentle heat. When melted, it should have a glossy, smooth consistency, and will easily set despite the added water. What can go wrong? Too much heat or cooking time and the chocolate will split and become grainy, dull and bitter.

ABOVE: Nasturtium, *Tropaeolum majus* 'Empress of India'.

15

16

17

18

19

20

21

22

23

24

25

26

27

28

SACHER TORTE

4 medium free range eggs at room temp
125g unsalted butter
75g sugar
125g 65/70% cocoa solids dark chocolate, broken into small pieces
125g ground almonds
2 tbsp of warmed apricot jam (use smooth jam or sieve out the fruit)

Topping
125g caster sugar
50g water
125g 65/70% cocoa solids dark chocolate
Small number of sugar or edible flowers

Separate the egg whites, and whip into stiff peaks. Set aside. Cream together the butter and sugar, then add the egg yolks. Melt the chocolate (see tip page 117) and add with the ground almonds. Mix thoroughly.

Carefully fold in the whisked egg whites, then transfer to a parchment lined 25cm baking tin. Cook at 150°C for 20–25 mins or until a skewer comes out clean. Allow to cool and turn out. Cover the top and sides with a thin layer of the apricot jam.

For the topping: in a small pan, heat the sugar and water together until the caramelisation has started, and the bubbling mix is a very light brown colour and slightly syrupy. Melt the chocolate as before, then add the sugar and water, stirring constantly.

Using a spatula, cover the Sacher Torte with a 2–3 mm thick layer of the chocolate and allow to set. Decorate with a small number of sugar or edible fresh flowers.

Viola 'Frosted Chocolate'.

BEEF AND ALE STEW

Serves 4
800g stewing beef, cubed
500ml Guinness or a similar dark ale
2 bay leaves
Sprig of thyme
2 tsp English mustard
100g seasoned flour
Olive oil
300g chopped onions
1 stick celery, chopped
12 small carrots
500ml beef stock
Dash of Worcestershire sauce
1 tbsp flat leaf parsley
Dash of Armagnac (optional)

Marinate the beef in the ale, bay leaves, thyme and mustard in the fridge overnight. Drain and remove the meat, setting aside the marinade. Toss the beef in the seasoned flour and brown in a pan with the oil. Remove the beef, then add the onions and celery to the pan until browned.

Next, combine in a clean pan, the beef, the onion and celery mix, the marinade and all the remaining ingredients except the Armagnac and half of the parsley. Bring just to the boil before turning down to a simmer, stirring occasionally to prevent any sticking. If the gravy shows signs of getting too viscous, top up with a little hot water.

Cook for 90 mins. The meat should be succulent and the gravy slightly thickened. Add the Armagnac, and simmer for a further 10 mins.

Serve with the remaining parsley, a hearty mash and some of your best Bordeaux.

Tangerine Dream Café Tip

29

30

31

ROASTING TOMATOES: Roasting tomatoes intensifies their taste and concentrates their properties. Tomatoes contain Lycopene, an antioxident with wide ranging health benefits for all ages.

Use good tomatoes! Grow your own or buy Italian plum vine tomatoes, splash on some good olive oil, generously salt, add a little pepper and finally a sprinkling of fresh thyme. Cook at 180°C for 20–30 mins, or until the edges are just browning. Ideal with a little green salad as an accompaniment to our savoury tart (see page 91).

ABOVE: A Garden visitor.
RIGHT: Tree tomato, *Solanum betaceum*, Tamarillo.

NOVEMBER

CHICKEN LIVER PATE

2 large banana shallots
1 clove of garlic
50g butter
500g chicken livers
3 tbsp brandy
2 tbsp double cream
1 dsp tomato purée
100g clarified butter (optional – for sealing top of
pate to preserve)

Fine chop the shallots and garlic. Sauté until lightly
caramelised in the butter. Remove from pan and
reserve. Pan fry the livers until just cooked, adding the
brandy half way through.

Combine the shallots, garlic, livers, cream and
tomato purée in a food processor and blend until
smooth. Press into a cling film lined dish or loaf tin
and refrigerate overnight. Covered, this will keep in
the fridge for several days.

To extend its life, cover with clarified butter before
refrigerating.

Serve with homemade chutney or cranberry relish,
rustic bread and a simple salad.

PREVIOUS PAGES: Looking south over the Systematic
Order Beds. The Monocotyledon *Yucca aloifolia* to the left.
OPPOSITE: Caught by a late afternoon sun the *Pterocarya
fraxinifolia* Caucasian wingnut.

1

2

3

4

5

6

7

8

9

10

11

12

13

14

CONFIT OF DUCK

Serves 4
1 large clove of fine chopped garlic
4 duck legs
5 tbsp sea salt
2 bay leaves, de-stalked
2 tsp dried thyme
Small pinch of dried parsley
500 – 600g of goose fat (or lard to substitute)

Rub the garlic into the surface of the duck. Scatter half of the salt into a dish, then lay the duck legs on top, skin side up. Chop the herbs together into a fine powder and scatter evenly over the duck, followed by the remainder of the salt. Refrigerate overnight, then turn the duck legs over and refrigerate for a further 12 hours. At this stage the salt should have liquefied.

Rinse the duck legs in cold water, and pat dry. Gently melt the goose fat in a casserole or oven proof dish and push the meat into the fat. The fat needs to cover the meat, so add extra fat as needed. Cook on the hob until just simmering, then transfer to an oven pre-heated to 150°C for 1.5 hours, or until tender.

Allow to cool slightly, then transfer the duck legs to an airtight container, sieving the fat over the meat. Take care not to add the meat juices – it's just the fat that you are after. Allow to cool, seal the top and refrigerate until required. Will keep for up to two weeks in an airtight container.

To serve, take the duck legs from the fridge and allow to come up to room temperature, then transfer to an oven pre-heated to 200°C and cook skin side up for 20 mins, by which time the skin should have become crisp. Ideal with truffle mash, a little red wine jus, or some parsley and garlic oil spooned over the skin.

Confit of duck leg poached in fat is at its best after a couple of weeks when the flavour will have fully developed.

LEFT: The Miller Beds with an old olive jar at the centre.
BELOW: *Asparagus officinalis.* Like many plants in the Garden, they are allowed to go to seed to provide new seeds for propagation.
OPPOSITE BELOW: *Cussonia baniculata* being put to bed for the winter.

Tangerine Dream Café Tip

ONIONS: Wet the onions with cold water to help prevent watering eyes. Cut the onion vertically into 2 halves. Core the base, then trim the top. Peel-off the outer hard layers, then place the halves flat on secure cutting board (use an anti-slip mat, or wet a spare dish cloth and place underneath your cutting board).

Use a sharp, not too wide bladed, 8" Cooks or Santoku knife held against the rounded face of your crooked forefinger and cut back across the onion as swiftly as you are comfortable with. The width of slice is regulated by the relaxing movement of your curled finger.

Practise makes perfect here, so don`t run before you can walk on the speed front, and don't drink alcohol before you do this! A sharp knife and confident cutting will reduce the eye watering effects of cutting onions to an absolute minimum.

15

16

17

18

19

20

21

22

23

24

25

26

27

28

ORANGE AND POLENTA CAKE

450g caster sugar
450g unsalted butter
450g ground almonds
1.5 tsp baking powder
6 large free range eggs
140g coarse polenta
Juice of 1 orange
Fine zest of 4 oranges

Blend together the sugar and butter. Add the ground almonds, baking powder and eggs, one at a time, then add the polenta and orange juice and zest, mixing well.

Line the base and sides of a 30cm spring-form cake tin with baking paper, pour in the mixture and bake for one hour at 150°C. Allow to cool before turning out and serve with a generous spoonful of crème fraîche.

To decorate, you can put a few caramelised oranges on top. Use one of the zested oranges that you will have left over.

Cut away the orange rind in six equal pieces, then cut the orange horizontally into 5mm slices. Heat up equal amounts of sugar and water by volume, sufficient to just cover the orange rind. Boil until just turning brown and thickening slightly. Place the orange slices in the pan, gently boiling for 5 mins. Allow to cool and remove the slices ready for use.

Citrus sinensis 'Moro Blood', a blood orange.

COQ AU VIN

Serves 4
Large free range chicken,
cut into 8 pieces
3 tbsp seasoned plain flour
60ml olive oil and butter mix
125g smoked streaky bacon,
sliced into strips
4 cloves garlic, rough chopped
200g button mushrooms
12 shallots, peeled and halved
750ml full-bodied and fruity red wine
12 small carrots
1 stick celery, diced
3 bay leaves
400ml chicken stock
Pinch dried chilli
2 tbsp parsley, chopped
Dash of brandy

Toss the chicken pieces in the seasoned flour until evenly coated, then fry off in a large pan with the butter and oil until browned. Fry 2 pieces of chicken at a time to get even colour and avoid any sticking. Set aside. Add the bacon to the pan, cook until browned but not crisped, then also set aside.

Add the garlic, mushrooms and shallots to the pan with a little of the wine, turn up the heat for a couple of minutes, sufficient to just de-glaze the pan when scraped with a flat wooden spoon. Transfer the contents to a large pot or Le Creuset style casserole dish. Add the chicken, carrots, celery, bay leaves, remaining wine, stock, chilli and half the parsley.

Bring to the boil, then simmer gently for at least an hour, adding the dash of brandy 15 mins before taking off the heat. The chicken should be fully cooked through, slipping easily off the bone, with the sauce turned to a thick gravy.

Serve with the remaining parsley, a hearty mash and some of your best Bordeaux wine.

Tangerine Dream Café Tip

29

30

CABBAGE: The first Savoy cabbages are reputedly to have come from Holland, and their name introduced to our language in the *Niewe Herball* by Henry Lyte in 1578. In general, avoid the temptation to overcook. Both cabbages and sprouts should retain their texture, not be boiled to a limp pulp which greatly reduces their taste. Overcooking also kills nutritional value in most vegetables.

Spring cabbage is best kept simple, but as autumn approaches you can be a bit more adventurous. Try almost dry-frying some bacon lardons in a shallow pan until browned before adding cooked cabbage or sprouts for 3–4 mins, turning constantly. Roasted and chopped chestnuts make an excellent addition to sprouts, particularly for Christmas lunch.

BELOW LEFT: Gardening materials, including a heavy lawn roller, in the Garden Stores.
BELOW: Cart describing the life and work of Carl Linnaeus (1707–1778). Linnaeus was a Swedish taxonomist and naturalist whose work *Systema naturae*, published in 1735, created a universal taxonomy of plants.

DECEMBER

1

2

3

4

5

6

7

PREVIOUS PAGES: Looking south east across the
Pharmaceutical Beds.
OPPOSITE: Cork oak, *Quercus suber*.
ABOVE TOP: Boot storage for the gardening staff.
BELOW: Common orange lichen, *Xanthoria parietina*, one
of a group of lichens used to make blue and purple dyes.

8

9

10

11

12

13

14

GAME STEW & GAME CHIPS

Serves 6
Stew
1.5 kg game mix – see your butcher, or combine venison, pigeon and pheasant
Seasoned flour, 250ml olive oil
400g shallots, finely chopped
3 cloves garlic, chopped
5 large carrots, chopped
8–10 juniper berries
Pinch of dried chilli flakes
2 x 1.5 ltr bottles full-bodied red wine
2 sticks of celery cut in 2cm slices
2 tbsp fresh parsley, chopped, 1 tbsp for dressing the plate
500ml vegetable stock
3 bay leaves

Chips
2 large beetroots, 1 large parsnip, 1 large Maris Piper potato, half a celeriac

Coat the game mix in the seasoned flour and fry in olive oil until brown. To keep the oil clean, do not cook too much at any one time. Transfer to a plate as each panful is cooked.

In a large stockpot gently simmer the shallots and garlic in olive oil until soft. Add the meat and the rest of the ingredients and simmer for at least an hour. Keep an eye on the liquid – it needs to develop to a thick gravy. Adjust with extra hot water as required.

For the chips: thinly slice all of the vegetables and shallow fry in hot sunflower oil until crisp. Pat dry on kitchen towel and salt generously.

Serve together with the game stew in a bowl, with a dash of cream or créme fraîche topping. This dish, like a good chilli, often improves on the second heating, so save a bit for the next day.

ABOVE: A welcoming Christmas wreath on the Royal Hospital Road entrance to the Garden.

RIGHT: Preserves and chutneys for sale from the café.

BELOW: Orange pomanders are easy to make. Take 500g of good quality cloves and 12 Moroccan oranges. Working round the outside of the orange push the complete clove gently into the skin, working in even lines with a small gap between each one. Leave in a warm place to dry, or on the mantelpiece where they will be a decorative seasonal addition.

Tangerine Dream Café Tip

ARTICHOKE CANDLESTICKS: Artichokes make a
sturdy and decorative base for candles, especially at
Christmas. Chop off the stem as close to the base as
possible. Using a sharp knife cut-out the centre to
create a hollow to take the candle of your choice.
Secure in place with melted wax.

15

16

17

18

19

20

21

22

23

24

25

26

27

28

CHRISTMAS CAKE

250g sultanas
250g chopped apricots
250g raisins
400ml strong cider
150ml whisky
225g unsalted butter
250g unrefined granulated sugar
Seeds from 10 cardamom pods
2 dsp ground cinnamon
Half a ground nutmeg
1 dsp allspice
2 tbsp/40ml treacle
50g dark chocolate, in small pieces
4 medium free range eggs, beaten
125g chopped mixed nuts
250g organic plain wholemeal flour
100g organic self raising white flour

Cover the dried fruit with 300ml of the cider and all the whisky and soak overnight.

When soaked, place in a saucepan with the butter, sugar, remaining cider and spices. Heat gently, stirring frequently until the butter has melted. Cook for a further 10 mins or so until the fruit has plumped up and the juices are thickened and syrupy. Remove from heat and stir in treacle and chocolate and leave to cool completely. Pre heat the oven to 120°C.

Beat the eggs into the fruit mixture, then stir in the nuts and flours until evenly combined. Line base and sides of a 25cm round cake tin with baking parchment and pour in the mixture, levelling off the surface. Wrap the tin in several thicknesses of newspaper to at least 1.5 times the height of the tin. This helps prevent the cake drying out during baking and keeps the fruit from burning (see tip p144).

Cook for 2 hours, or until it has attained a firm texture, and a skewer comes out clean.

Wrapped in parchment and foil this cake will last 6 – 8 weeks in a cool environment. To keep it moist, unwrap the top and feed with a couple of tablespoons of cider/whisky mix every 2 weeks.

Decorate with crystallised fruits and a festive ribbon.

CHOCOLATE TRUFFLES

Makes 40
375g 65/70% cocoa solids dark chocolate
80g softened butter, cubed
Cocoa for coating
40g finely chopped nuts (optional)

Break chocolate into pieces and melt (see tip page 117). Keep the water simmering and stir chocolate until smooth.

Slowly add the butter a cube at a time, until well combined and smooth. Add the chopped nuts and stir to combine.

Cover the bowl and refrigerate for one hour until the mixture is firm.

To make the truffles, roll 2 teaspoons of mixture into a ball, roll in cocoa and place on a plate. When all the balls are formed cover the plate and refrigerate until firm.

Refrigerated they will keep for one week.

Tangerine Dream Café Tip

When cooking the Christmas cake, wrapping the tin in newspaper and tying with string helps keep the cake moist and stops it from burning.

29

30

31

ABOVE: Crucifixion thorn or anchor plant, *Colletia paradoxa.*
BELOW: The Sir Hans Sloane statue festooned with a seasonal garland for the Garden's Christmas Fair. In the background, one of a pair of *Ginkgo biloba* trees which border either side of the walk to the Chelsea Embankment gate.

FLAMING CHRISTMAS PUDDING

Serves 8 –10

175g sultanas

175g raisins

125g chopped candied peel

110g soft dried figs, rough chopped

110g dark candied cherries, halved

150ml brandy

Juice and zest of 1 orange

3 large free range eggs, lightly beaten

125g shredded suet

1 carrot coarsely grated

3 tbsp black treacle

175g dark muscovado sugar

125g fresh breadcrumbs

110g self raising flour

1 tsp mixed spice

Put the dried fruit in a bowl with the brandy for approx 12 hours stirring occasionally.

Mix the orange zest and juice, eggs, suet and carrot in a bowl. Stir in the treacle, sugar, breadcrumbs, flour and mixed spice. Fold in the mixed fruit, then pour the mix into a lightly buttered 1.5–1.75 ltr china pudding basin.

Cut a piece of baking parchment to fit round the top of the basin and down the sides. Do the same with a piece of muslin. A section of old linen tea towel will substitute. Lightly butter the underside of the baking parchment, then fold a pleat across the centre and secure round the rim of the bowl with string. Cover with the muslin, and again secure with string.

Gently lower the bowl into a large pan half filled with boiling water and cover with a lid. Allow to simmer for 3.5 hours, topping up with boiling water from a kettle as the water level gets low.

Once cooled this will store up to 3 months in a cool dark place. To serve, re-heat in the same fashion for 2.5–3 hours, then turn out onto a large plate, and cover with 2 tablespoons of well warmed brandy which can be lit as the pudding comes to the table. Spectacular with either brandy butter or cream.

This is a dark traditional pudding dating from the Victorian age, made with black treacle and figs.

MULLED WINE

4 bottles of full-bodied red wine, not too dry. We like a Cabernet Sauvignon and Argentinian Malbec mix
500ml fresh orange juice
250ml ruby port
125ml brandy – a moderate quality is fine
2 cinnamon sticks
2 blood oranges, studded with cloves
1 tsp allspice
2 bay leaves

Add all of the contents to a large stock pot and heat gently, do not allow to boil otherwise the alcohol will steam off. Keep at low heat for 10 mins, then cool, which gives the spices time to steep.

Keep for at least 2 hours before serving. Serve warm with mince pies and brandy butter. May be re-heated. Keeps in a fridge or cool larder for 2 days.

SLOE VODKA

Makes 2 x 1 litre bottles
2 litres of vodka or gin as a substitute
800g caster sugar
600g wild sloes
2 empty 1 litre bottles

Pick the sloes as late as possible in the season. Ideally the fruit should be firm when picked but not hard, and should have been subject to a light frost. If this is not the case put the fruit in the freezer overnight to achieve the same result.

Prick the fruit lightly before placing equal quantities of sugar and fruit in each bottle, topping up with vodka or gin.

Cork the bottles and shake vigorously to begin dissolving the sugar. Give the bottles a good shake every couple of days until the sugar has been fully absorbed into the mix, then lay the bottles down in a cool dark place for at least three months.

The sloes will gradually diffuse into the mix increasing the intensity of the flavour for up to a year. Keep an eye on your bottles having a small nip at periodic intervals after the first three months to find your preferred taste. Add 50g of sugar to sweeten if desired.

It is recommended that the fruit is filtered out after a year as it often begins to break down slightly, reducing the purity of the finished result.

Delicious when served on ice.